P9-ELP-742

A Troll First-Start® Tall Tale

John Henry
AND HIS MIGHTY HAMMER

by Patsy Jensen • illustrated by Roseanne Litzinger

Troll Associates

Property of NCS Library

The John Henry in this story is a pretend person. But there may have been a real John Henry long ago. Some say he was born in Tennessee and died in 1870. And they say there really was a race between John Henry and a steam drill.

A tall tale is an unusual story that has been exaggerated as it is retold over the years. If there was a real John Henry, he probably wasn't quite as strong as the stories tell. The important thing to remember, though, is the spirit of John Henry, that tells us, "I can do this job, and I can do it well."

Copyright © 1994 by Troll Associates. No part of this book may be used or reproduced in any manner whatsoever without written permission of the publisher.

Printed in the United States of America.

10 9 8 7 6 5 4 3 2 1

John Henry was the biggest, fastest,
strongest steel-driving man that ever lived.

People say that John Henry was born
with a hammer in his hand. But that is not
true. He did not pick up a hammer until he
was three weeks old.

People also say that right after John Henry was born, he said to his mama and daddy, "I am a steel-driving man. And I will die with a hammer in my hand." But that also is not true.

He actually said, "I'm hungry."

For John Henry's first meal, he ate three sides of beef, three pots of mashed potatoes, fifty ears of corn, and ten apple pies for dessert.

Not bad for a ten-minute-old baby.

When he was four weeks old, John Henry started swinging his daddy's hammer against some rocks.

"I'm a steel-driving man," he said. "And I will die with a hammer in my hand."

John Henry's mama frowned at his words. "I don't want you to be a steel-driving man," she said. "You had better find something else to do."

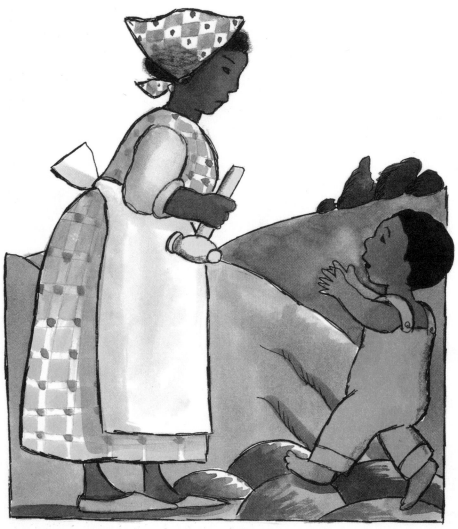

And so John Henry stopped swinging his
daddy's hammer.

But John Henry did not stop growing. He
grew and grew, and then he grew some more.

When he got older, John Henry did lots of things. He picked cotton and tobacco. He loaded crates and barrels onto ships. He was a mule driver.

But John Henry never felt as good as he did with a hammer in his hand.

13

One day John Henry saw a beautiful young woman.

Her name was Polly Ann. She and John Henry took a liking to each other. Soon they got married.

"There is something I must tell you," he said to Polly Ann after their wedding. "I'm a steel-driving man. And I will die with a hammer in my hand."

Polly Ann didn't say a word. She knew that John Henry would not be happy unless he was swinging a hammer.

John Henry and Polly Ann headed to West Virginia, where railroads were being built.

"There is work to be done," said John Henry. "And I'm just the steel-driving man to do it."

Sure enough, they soon heard the sound of hammers ringing against steel. The wagon headed around one last bend, and John Henry was greeted with a beautiful sight.

There in the valley below were hundreds of men, hammering and singing. They were building the Big Bend Tunnel for the Chesapeake and Ohio Railroad. The tunnel was going to go right through a big mountain.

John Henry headed right over to the boss. His name was Captain Tommy.

"Captain," said John Henry, "I am here to drive steel for you."

Captain Tommy only had to take one look at John Henry to see that this was the biggest, strongest, fastest steel-driving man around.

Of course, John Henry did not use a ten-pound hammer like the other men. His hammer weighed thirty pounds, and no other man could swing it.

But one woman could swing it. Every now and then, when John Henry came down with a cold, Polly Ann would take his place. And it was said that she drove steel almost as fast as John Henry.

One day a man in fancy clothes came to the railroad camp. He brought a strange machine.

"This is a steam drill," he told Captain Tommy. "It can outdrill five men in half the time."

Captain Tommy just laughed. "I do not need five men to beat your machine. I have one man here who can do it."

The two men made a bet. Who could drill faster—the steam drill or John Henry?

"No machine can beat a steel-driving man," said John Henry. "I will prove it."

The man turned on the steam drill. John Henry picked up his great hammer. The race began.

Hour after hour, the steam drill kept going. So did John Henry.

"Who is winning?" John Henry finally asked.

"It's about even," said Captain Tommy.

"No machine can even tie a steel-driving man," said John Henry.

He picked up a second thirty-pound hammer. He began swinging both hammers with all his might.

Finally the judge blew the whistle. The race was over. John Henry was the winner!

John Henry smiled as the railroad workers cheered. Then he laid down, with a hammer in his hand.

"I am tired," said John Henry. "But I beat the machine, just like I said I would." Then he closed his eyes and died.

Polly Ann buried John Henry near the Big Bend Tunnel. And she buried him with a hammer in his hand.